Girls Science Club

Cool Physics Activities for Girls

by Suzanne Slade

Consultant:
Susan K. Blessing
Professor of Physics
Florida State University
Tallahassee, Florida

CAPSTONE PRESS
a capstone imprint

Snap Books are published by Capstone Press,
1710 Roe Crest Drive, North Mankato, Minnesota 56003.
www.capstonepub.com

Copyright © 2012 by Capstone Press, a Capstone imprint.
All rights reserved.
No part of this publication may be reproduced in whole or in part, or stored in a retrieval system,
or transmitted in any form or by any means, electronic, mechanical, photocopying, recording,
or otherwise, without written permission of the publisher.
For information regarding permission, write to Capstone Press,
1710 Roe Crest Drive, North Mankato, Minnesota 56003.

 Books published by Capstone Press are manufactured with paper containing at least 10 percent post-consumer waste.

Library of Congress Cataloging-in-Publication Data
Slade, Suzanne.
Cool physics activities for girls / by Suzanne Slade.
  p. cm.—(Snap books. Girls science club)
Includes bibliographical references and index.
Summary: "Provides step-by-step instructions for activities demonstrating physics concepts
and scientific explanations of the concepts presented"—Provided by publisher.
ISBN 978-1-4296-7675-5 (library binding)
ISBN 978-1-4296-8022-6 (paperback)
1. Physics projects—Juvenile literature. 2. Physics—Experiments—Juvenile literature.
3. Girls—Education—Juvenile literature. I. Title.
QC25.S48 2012
530.076—dc23   2011020702

Editor: Jennifer Besel
Designer: Heidi Thompson
Photo Stylist: Sarah Schuette
Scheduler: Marcy Morin
Production Specialist: Kathy McColley

Photo Credits:
Photos by Capstone Studio: Karon Dubke, except iStockphoto Inc: DSGpro, cover (top), Mark Evans, cover (bottom);
Shutterstock: blue67design, cover (drawn design), wavebreakmedia ltd, 5

Printed in the United States of America in North Mankato, Minnesota.
052017   010512R

Table of Contents

Not a Secret Anymore! 4
Waving Magnets 6
Floating Needle 8
Impossible Water Trick 10
Party Punch Trick 12
Floating Party Drinks 14
Disappearing Sticks 16
Magic Divers 18
Mysterious Balancing Can 20
Defying Gravity 22
Floating Ping-Pong Ball 24
Dancing Slime 26

Glossary 30
Read More 31
Internet Sites 31
Index 32

Not a Secret Anymore!

Waving magnets. Dancing slime. Floating soda cans. This isn't magic. It's physics! Discover a secret that scientists have known for years—physics is fun!

Physics is a branch of science that studies matter and how it moves. Matter is the stuff that makes up everything in the world. Things that make matter move or change shape are called forces. And forces give matter energy. Physicists study all these pieces to understand how our world works. So what are you waiting for? Get your matter moving!

To have the most fun with these projects, just follow a few simple guidelines:
1. Read the project all the way through before you start.
2. Gather all the materials you need.
3. If you don't get the results you expect the first time, try it again. The experiment might work a different way the next time.
4. Have fun!

Waving Magnets

Can you make an object move without touching it? Maybe your magnetic personality, or two strong magnets, will do the trick!

Supplies

- 2 round magnets about the size of quarters and ¼ inch (.64 centimeter) thick
- pencil

1. Move the magnets together to find the sides that pull toward each other.

2. Pull the magnets apart. Put a small pencil dot on the sides that had been pressed together.

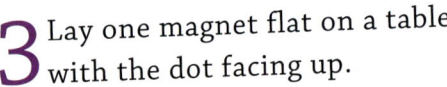

3. Lay one magnet flat on a table with the dot facing up.

4 Stand the second magnet upright on its thin edge. Face the dot away from the other magnet.

5 Slowly slide the upright magnet toward the magnet lying flat. Keep sliding until the flat magnet begins to move and wave.

Insider Info

Every magnet has two opposite **poles**, called north and south. Magnets attract each other when their opposite poles face each other. Magnets **repel** each other when their same poles face each other.

As you slid the upright magnet near the other magnet, their same sides moved toward each other. When the magnets got close, the poles repelled each other. Soon, the magnet on the table lifted up. After it lifted off the table, the sides with the opposite poles faced each other. They attracted, and the table magnet moved down. When the magnet was down, the same sides of the magnets faced each other again. So the magnet rose. This cycle of attraction and repelling continued, causing the table magnet to wave up and down.

pole: one of the two ends of a magnet
repel: to push apart

Floating Needle

Metal objects always sink in water, right? Well, not always. With a little patience, and a lot of help from water **molecules**, you can make a metal needle float!

Supplies

- glass drinking cup
- water
- needle
- fork
- liquid dish soap

1. Fill a cup three-fourths full of water.

2. Place a dry needle across the fork's tines. Slowly lower the fork into the water. Keep the needle even so one end isn't lower than the other.

3 As you lower the fork below the water's surface, the needle should float on top of the water. If the needle doesn't float the first time, catch it with the fork. Lift it to the surface of the water, and try again. Once the needle is floating, slowly remove the fork.

4 Put a drop of dish soap on your finger. Hold your hand just above the glass, and let the soap drip from your finger into the water. What happens to the needle now?

Insider Info

A cup of water contains trillions of tiny water molecules. Each water molecule is made of two hydrogen atoms and one oxygen atom. The side of a water molecule with the oxygen atom has a negative **charge**. The side with the two hydrogen atoms has a positive charge. Just like magnets, the negative side of a water molecule is attracted to the positive side of another molecule. The attraction between molecules on the top of water is called surface tension. The surface tension creates a strong film of water. This film kept the needle from falling. Dish soap disrupts the attraction between water molecules and breaks the surface tension. It doesn't take much to disrupt the attraction. Just one drop of soap made the needle fall.

molecule: the atoms making up the smallest unit of a substance; H_2O is a molecule of water

charge: a measure of electricity

Impossible Water Trick

Do your friends trust you? Test their trust by asking them to let you turn a glass of water upside down over their heads. No one will get wet. But will they chicken out before you get the chance to prove it?

Supplies

- glass drinking cup
- water
- plastic lid from a small container

1. Carefully fill the glass to the very top with water. The water level needs to bulge slightly above the sides of the glass.

2. Lay the plastic lid on top of the glass so it covers the opening.

3. Hold the lid firmly down on the glass. Then turn the glass and lid upside down.

4 Hold the glass tightly as you slowly take your hand away from the lid.

5 Watch as the lid mysteriously holds the water inside the glass.

6 Place your finger on the lid before turning the glass back over.

Insider Info

The key to this trick is all around you—air. Although you can't see air, this **gas** really knows how to throw its weight around. The weight of air is always pushing on everything it touches. This weight is called air **pressure**. In this activity one side of the plastic lid is against the water. The other side is exposed to air. Only the side facing the air has air pressure pushing on it. That air pressure holds up the lid, keeping the water inside the glass.

gas: something that is not solid or liquid and does not have a definite shape
pressure: a force that pushes on something

Party Punch Trick

Candles add a certain flair to parties. But when the celebration is over, you need to put out the candles. Surprise your friends by having physics put out the candles for you!

Supplies

- liquid measuring cup
- ½ cup (120 mL) punch or water
- glass pie plate
- tea light candle
- candle lighter
- small glass drinking cup

1. Measure and pour the punch or water into the pie plate.

2. Put the candle in the center of the plate.

3. Ask an adult to help you light the candle.

4. To put out the flame, place the open end of the glass over the candle and down on the plate.

5. Watch as the liquid rises inside the glass and the candle goes out!

Insider Info

After covering the burning candle, the flame used up the oxygen gas in the glass. The reduced amount of gas created a lower air pressure in the glass than outside the glass. Gas always moves from higher pressure to lower pressure. The only way the high-pressure air outside the glass could move inside was to go under the glass. This air movement created **suction**. Suction pulled the punch under the cup, and put out the candle.

suction: the act of drawing air out of a space to create a vacuum, causing the surrounding air or liquid to be sucked into the empty space

Floating Party Drinks

Serving soda at your next party? Here's a way to show off the beverage selection in style. You'll also discover a little about what's inside your soda as you watch the cans sink or swim!

Supplies

- liquid measuring cup
- water
- large bowl
- food coloring, blue and red
- spoon
- 4 ice cube trays
- large clear container for cans to float inside
- at least 4 cans of diet soda
- at least 4 cans of regular soda

 **TIP:** A clear drawer from your refrigerator or an empty aquarium work well to hold the soda cans and water.

1. At least six hours before your party, make colorful ice cubes. Measure 4 cups (960 mL) water into a large bowl. Put six drops of blue food coloring into the water and stir. Carefully pour the water into two ice cube trays. Place the trays in the freezer. Repeat with the other two trays and the red coloring.

2. After they're frozen, add some of the colored ice cubes to the large, clear container. Save some cubes so you can add them later to keep the soda cool.

3 Place the soda cans inside the container.

4 Fill the container about half way with water. Watch as some of the cans begin to float.

Insider Info

Why did some cans sink and others float? To answer that question, you have to understand density. Density is how much **mass** an object has in a certain amount of space. Every object has some density. But objects of the same size can have very different densities. For example, compare a bowling ball and a basketball. The balls take up the same amount of space. But the bowling ball is denser because it has more mass packed into that space than the basketball.

So how does this relate to the soda cans? The cans of regular soda didn't float because the soda inside is more dense than the water. This high density comes from the sugar in regular soda. Diet sodas contain chemical sweetener instead of heavy sugar. The diet soda is less dense than water, so those cans float.

mass: the amount of material in an object

Disappearing Sticks

Now you see it, now you don't! Astound your classmates and science teacher with this disappearing act you can do in your school lab. Just make sure you get the items to reappear before the bell rings!

Supplies

- 2 small clear glass or plastic bowls
- water
- vegetable oil
- **Pyrex** stirring stick
- small Pyrex beaker

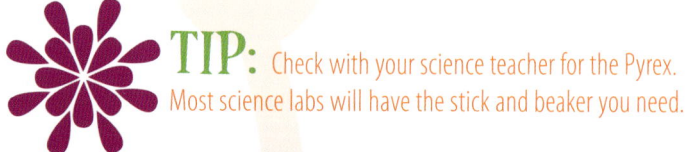

TIP: Check with your science teacher for the Pyrex. Most science labs will have the stick and beaker you need.

1. Fill one bowl about three-fourths full with water.

2. Fill the second bowl about three-fourths full with oil.

3. Place the Pyrex stick in the water. Can you see the stick in the water?

4 Place the Pyrex stick in the oil. Can you see it in the oil?

5 Now slowly lower the beaker into the oil, and watch it vanish!

Insider Info

Light bends as it goes through an object or substance. We see objects because our eyes detect that bending light. Scientists call the measure of how much a light ray bends the object's index of refraction. In this activity you could see the Pyrex stick in the water. You saw it because the Pyrex's index of refraction is different from the water's index of refraction. When light traveled through the water into the stick, the light waves bent. Your eyes saw those bending light rays.

The Pyrex stick and beaker seemed to disappear in the oil. The indexes of refraction of Pyrex and vegetable oil are about the same. So as light rays moved through the oil into the Pyrex they didn't bend. The Pyrex was invisible to your eyes.

Pyrex: a type of glass that is resistant to heat, chemicals, and electricity

Magic Divers

You can't always get people to do what you say. But in this activity, you can make a ketchup diver sink and rise at your command. All you need is a sly movement of your hand and a little help from science.

Supplies

- large bowl
- water
- 6 or more small ketchup packets
- 2-liter soda bottle with lid, label removed

1. Fill the bowl about half full of water.

2. Place all the ketchup packets in the bowl of water. Some packets might sink, others will float. Choose a packet that just barely floats above the surface. Use this packet for the activity.

3. Fill the 2-liter bottle to the very top with water.

4. Over the sink, push the ketchup packet you selected inside the bottle. A little water will spill out.

5. Put the lid on the bottle and tighten.

6. Squeeze the bottle near the base, and watch the packet dive! Let go, and the packet will float back up. Make your magic diver dance by squeezing and unsqueezing the bottle.

Insider Info

This project is called a Cartesian diver. Pressure and density are the secrets that make it work. When you squeezed the bottle, you increased the water pressure in the bottle. The increased pressure squeezed the air pocket inside the ketchup packet. With a smaller air pocket, the packet became more dense. When the density of the ketchup packet became greater than the density of water, the packet sank.

Why did you have to carefully choose which packet to use? Ketchup packets don't have the same amount of air in them. The packets that floated high above the water's surface had more air in them. They would require more water pressure to make them sink. The sinking packets weren't a good choice either. They had so little air they were already sinking.

Mysterious Balancing Can

You can't balance a soda can on one edge, right? Actually, with a little physics, you can. Make your friends think a ghost stopped by with this spooky balancing can.

Supplies
- empty soda can
- water

1 Fill an empty soda can about one-third full of water.

2 Try balancing the can on one edge.

3 Add or remove water until the can balances by itself.

4 Give the can a gentle push so it rolls on its edge. Surprise! The can doesn't tip over!

Insider Info

Center of **gravity** (cg) is the key to this balancing act. Cg is the place where the force of gravity pulls down on an object. For an object to be balanced, its weight needs to be evenly distributed around its cg. The cg in an empty soda can is in the center of the can. If you try to balance it on an edge, the can falls. It isn't balanced on its cg, and the force of gravity pulls it down.

Adding water to the can adds weight to the bottom. The weight of the water shifts the can's cg to a lower point. The can stays upright on its edge because it's balancing on a point directly below its new cg. You can roll the can on its edge because the water moves as the can moves. The flowing water keeps the cg at the same point.

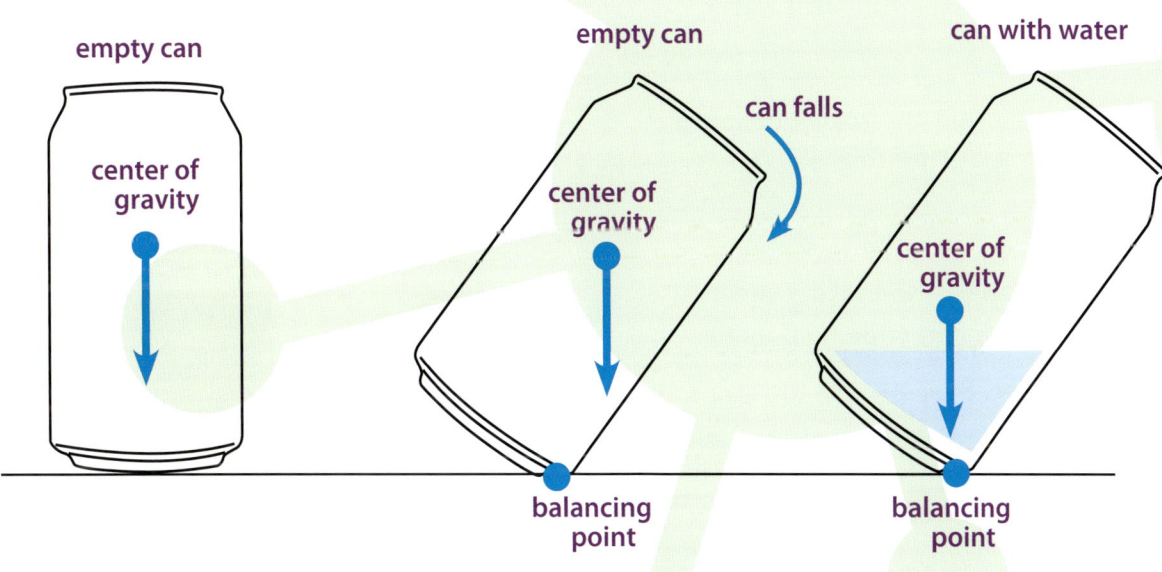

gravity: a force that pulls objects down toward the center of earth

Defying Gravity

No doubt about it, gravity is a powerful force. It pulls everything down, including the drink in your cup. So what will your friends think when you seem to defy gravity with this fun trick?

Supplies

- two short glasses of the same size
- water
- food coloring, any color
- spoon
- scissors
- paper towel
- ruler

1 Fill one glass a little more than three-fourths full with water.

2 Add four or five drops of coloring to the water. Stir.

3 Cut the paper towel into a square 6 inches (15 cm) wide by 6 inches (15 cm) long.

4 Roll the square towel into a tight tube. Twist the ends of the paper towel so it stays in its tube shape.

5 Set your two glasses side by side. Place one end of the paper tube in the glass filled with water. Bend the tube over so the other end is in the empty glass.

6 Now sit back and watch. In a few hours both glasses will have the same amount of water.

Insider Info

Gravity doesn't let go in this experiment. It's just overridden for a while. The water molecules' positive and negative sides stuck to each other in the glass. But the water molecules were also attracted to the paper's fiber molecules. So the "sticky" water molecules pulled each other up the paper towel tube. This movement against gravity through a tube is called capillary action.

When the water in the tube got to the side of the empty glass, gravity took over. It pulled the water down into the glass. Capillary action and gravity moved the water until both glasses had the same amount of water. Then the water stopped moving. Why? Because the system became balanced. By the time both glasses had the same amount of water, both sides of the tube were full of water. Gravity could then pull down on the same amount of water on each side of the tube.

23

Floating Ping-Pong Ball

A hair dryer can be a girl's best friend. But this BFF can also be a big hit at your next gathering. Grab your trusty dryer, and get ready to amaze your friends!

Supplies

- hair dryer with a cool setting
- Ping-Pong ball
- cardboard toilet paper tube

1. Plug in your hair dryer. Turn on the dryer. Use the cool temperature setting and high airflow setting.

2. Point the hair dryer up. Place a Ping-Pong ball in the air stream above the hair dryer.

3. Hold the dryer still as the ball floats and spins.

4. Move the dryer slightly right and left. Watch as the ball moves to follow the air stream.

5. Now position the hair dryer so the ball is directly above the dryer again.

6 Hold a toilet paper tube above the ball, and watch the ball take off through the tube!

Insider Info

Daniel Bernoulli was a scientist who made fascinating discoveries about moving air. One of his discoveries, now called Bernoulli's Principle, helps explain what happens in this experiment. Bernoulli's Principle says that the faster air moves past a surface, the lower the air pressure on that surface. The air coming out of your hair dryer moved quickly around the Ping-Pong ball. As this fast-moving air sped past the ball, it created an area of low pressure. The air surrounding the dryer's air stream wasn't moving. This non-moving air created high pressure that pushed in on the ball. The differing pressures pushed against each other, keeping the ball inside the moving air stream.

When the air traveled into the toilet paper tube, it moved even faster. The faster air created an even lower pressure area than the air surrounding the ball. This difference in air pressure pulled the ball into the tube.

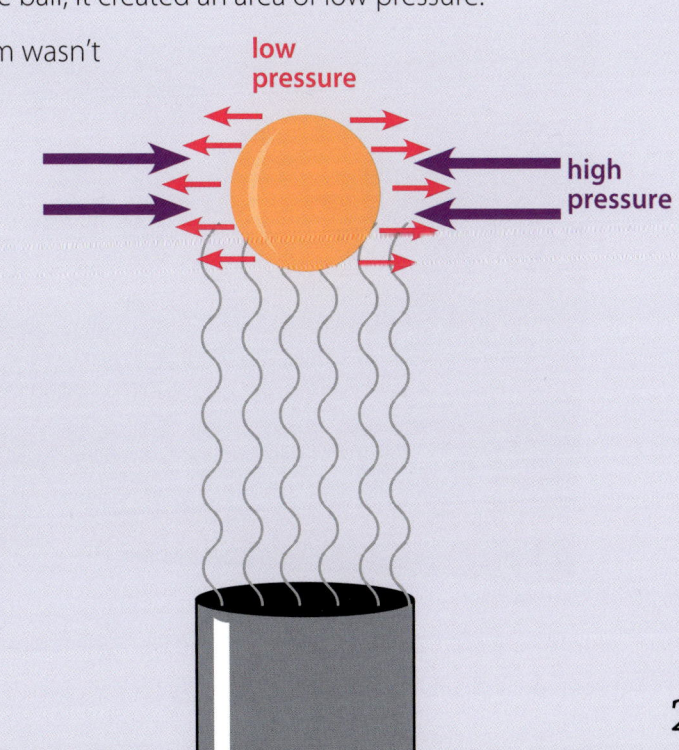

Dancing Slime

What's more fun than slime? Dancing slime, of course! Get ready to make some colorful slime bust a move to hip hoppin' beats.

Supplies

- measuring spoons
- spoon
- 6 level tablespoons (90 mL) cornstarch
- 3 tablespoons (45 mL) water
- 2 small bowls
- yellow and green food coloring
- old bed sheet
- speaker with exposed **woofer** (Subwoofers work best.)
- plastic wrap
- clear tape
- **receiver** with a music source such as a CD or MP3 player
- straw (optional)

woofer: a round, plastic part on the speaker which vibrates when music plays

receiver: a piece of electronic equipment that converts signals to audio form

Part 1: Make the Slime

1. Measure and mix the cornstarch and water in a small bowl. Slowly stir the mixture until the cornstarch is dissolved. The slime mixture should look runny. But when you move your finger through it quickly, the mixture will become stiff.

2. Pour half the slime mixture into another bowl. Add one drop of green food coloring to one of the bowls. Stir until the color is mixed in. Do the same with the yellow food coloring in the other bowl.

Part 2: Make a rocking Slime Studio

1. Lay an old sheet over the floor or table where you're working. Set the speaker on the sheet with the woofer facing up.

2. Cover the entire front of the speaker with clear plastic wrap. Make sure the plastic is loose enough that it sinks down and lies on top of the woofer.

continue on next page

3 Securely tape the edges of the plastic wrap to the speaker.

4 Have an adult help you connect the speaker to a receiver with a CD player or other music source.

5 Drop a spoonful of each colored slime onto the plastic-covered woofer.

6 Turn on a song with a great bass beat. Crank up the bass and turn up the volume to see your slime dance! If your slime is a little shy, blow on it through a straw to help get it started.

Insider Info

The slime you created is called a non-Newtonian fluid. A non-Newtonian fluid doesn't follow Isaac Newton's rules of how a fluid should behave. It doesn't always stay runny and flow. A non-Newtonian fluid acts like a liquid when it is under low **stress**. But under high stress, it acts like a solid.

So why did your slime dance? The sound waves created quick, high stresses. These stresses made the slime act like a solid and hold a shape. Between the sound waves, the slime was not under stress and became smooth and runny. To understand why this happens, take a closer look at your slime. The cornstarch and water molecules didn't actually combine to make a new solution. The tiny solid pieces of cornstarch were floating around in the water. A quick stress squeezed the water molecules out from between the cornstarch molecules. The water moved away, leaving behind a damp cornstarch solid. Once the stress was gone, the water flowed back between the cornstarch molecules to create runny slime.

stress: physical pressure, pull, or other force on an object

Glossary

charge (CHARJ)—a measure of electricity

gas (GASS)—something that is not solid or liquid and does not have a definite shape

gravity (GRAV-uh-tee)—a force that pulls objects with mass together; gravity pulls objects down toward the center of earth

mass (MASS)—the amount of material in an object

molecule (MOL-uh-kyool)—the atoms making up the smallest unit of a substance; H_2O is a molecule of water

pole (POHL)—one of the two ends of a magnet; a pole can also be the top or bottom part of a planet

pressure (PRESH-ur)—a force that pushes on something

Pyrex (PI-reks)—a type of glass that is specially created to be resistant to heat, chemicals, and electricity

receiver (ree-SEE-vuhr)—a piece of electronic equipment that converts signals to audio form

repel (ri-PEL)—to push apart

stress (STRESS)—the physical pressure, pull, or other force on an object

suction (SUHK-shuhn)—the act of drawing air out of a space to create a vacuum, causing the surrounding air or liquid to be sucked into the empty space

woofer (WUF-uhr)—a round, plastic part on the speaker which vibrates when music plays

Read More

Bell-Rehwoldt, Sheri. *Science Experiments that Surprise and Delight: Fun Projects for Curious Kids.* Kitchen Science. Mankato, Minn.: Capstone Press, 2011.

Mills, J. Elizabeth. *The Everything Kids' Easy Science Experiments Book: Explore the World of Science Through Quick and Fun Experiments.* Everything Kids'. Avon, Mass.: Adams Media, 2010.

Williams, Zella. *Experiments with Physical Science.* Do-It-Yourself Science. New York: PowerKids Press, 2007.

Internet Sites

FactHound offers a safe, fun way to find Internet sites related to this book. All of the sites on FactHound have been researched by our staff.

Here's all you do:

Visit www.facthound.com

Type in this code: 9781429676755

Check out projects, games and lots more at www.capstonekids.com

Index

air pressure, 11, 13, 25

Bernoulli's Principle, 25

capillary action, 23
Cartesian divers, 18–19
center of gravity, 21

density, 15, 19

gravity, 21, 22–23

indexes of refraction, 17

light, 17

magnets, 4, 6–7, 9
mass, 15
matter, 4
molecules, 8–9, 23

non-Newtonian fluid, 4, 26–29

slime. *See* non-Newtonian fluid
sound waves, 29
suction, 13
surface tension, 9

water pressure, 19